# ICE FISHING
## by
## Frank Kooistra

## *Dedication*

### A Childless Couple's Vietnam Adoption Wishes

Old enemy, can you spare a child?
Just a very small one, meek and mild.

We will be the parents, she and I,
And he will be an American, by and by.

We are not visited on you as napalm—
After such a long war, now peace and calm.

We would like to say we're sorry
And we can do this without worry

Because you let the war go as the past.
May our love for you last and last.

---

### (c) 2004 by Frank Kooistra
### ISBN 0-914720-14-7
### $5.95

*A Cave Horse Book*
186 Pegasus Drive, NW
Dover, OH 44622
*www.palehorsepress.com*

# Diesel

The smell of the exhaust was unmistakable,
And truck or fishing boat, I am carried back
As if I were hearing Lawrence's booming piano wires,
Not to childhood, but to the world of work,
Which is what I remember best.

We would cruise out of harbor
Before daybreak trailing black exhaust,
Diesel exhaust mixed with a cold sea breeze,
And it was diesel all day, blended
With the blood smell of salmon,
Red ocean flesh and black particulate matter.
Diesel power was reliable, and the hold would fill,
Hundreds upon hundreds of fish hauled in
By a mindlessly persistent engine,
Moodless, always ready to work,
Asking no thanks for what it could do.

We never thought we were taking advantage,
Never considered we had an edge
On an ungrudging ocean.

You did the work of many horses
And brought money in over the transom,
Kept your skipper comfortably through the year,
And then,
Dry-docked, stored on land for the winter,
You started at the first turn of the key,
The screw turning in air,
Ready for more hundreds of hours of running
As the yellow crane lifted you high in the air
And set you gently in the tidal river.

## Woman With Child in Her Arms, Standing Outside the Hotel

Her auxiliary husband stands to one side
As she holds her small son in her arms,
His head cradled against her shoulder;
They talk softly, only loud enough
For both to hear, and the world falls away
On either side of them, nothing of importance
On the periphery. Even the blazing sun
Falling out of its prominent place in the sky
Would be of small concern to what they say
To each other, the sole occupants of the
Known universe, around which every star
And planet turns. You say you believe
In music of the spheres? What our ears
Can't hear is being sung here, curbside.

# End of the Fishing Season – Ninilchik, Alaska

In front of newly-built front steps, fresh wood nailed
To flaking red siding, built for my brother's family,
We, my brother's wife and I, watch the host of purple martins
Crisscross cat's cradle-like among the swarms of mosquitoes
Clouding up when the sea breeze slackens at twilight.
Her husband, my brother sits anchored on the other side
Of the inlet, fishing for beach-running cohos
Which bring a good price during the warm autumnal afternoons
Of late August, when days are wide and dry,
And bald eagles perch in the deadwood above the beach,
Screaming as they cross the gray pebbled, tide-out shore,
Battening on the apoplectic red flanks of watermarked salmon,
Fish gone home to sweet water in the creeks but
Mysteriously come back out, turned to ruby in the ocean.
My brother steps off the deck of the fishing boat
And rows to shore, pulling net in his skiff,
And he crunches across gravel dragging net with him,
Fishing illegally, netting silvers protected in the beach run.
Those extra fifty fish will buy something real,
Gas or food or car parts; they are as tangible as folding money,
And drop into the hold as the martins fly away in
Semi-darkness, making room for the bats which squeak
On leather wings, gobbling insects in their turn.
My brother's wife gathers her grubby children
In her thin strong arms, plucks them off tricycles
In the roadside dust and carries them inside.
A lone light bulb shines in the kitchen, the glow
Feebled by snowcapped volcanoes darkening to rose
In the midnight twilight on the northwest shore,
Where eagles sit their perches and watch and sleep.

# The Poet's Function

The surgeon on board with us, taking in
A day's fishing, lectures about healing,
Pointing to the cut side and open wound
On a salmon's flank (caught and cut in
Another fisherman's net somewhere, no doubt);
He tells us that a red wound filling
In with pale new flesh is called
A "granulating wound," or "granulation."
And granulation is what poets do best.

Beneath the wreckage of Tokyo and Berlin
In pools of warming rain water the frog poets
Began to sing, first the peeps and then
The chorus, their voices ballooning
Like frog throats, celebrating life
Where all things were ruined, but still there.

## March Light and Dark

It's bales, clouds in bales
Which blot out and let in the sun,
As if sky were an old cotton exchange
Hurrying to load its goods on ship,
And we the slaves who watch the ships go,
Not without a pang, to freer places.

# The Artist Edward Hopper
# And The Interstate

You would know Dairy Mart when the sky is still dark
With tatters of gauze-white clouds and distant starlight,
And the gas pumps a big blaze of light,
People inside standing in line to buy coffee
And the rest of the morning's start, donuts, papers,
Lottery tickets—you would understand lottery tickets,
Or you would know the loneliness of the road
When the city thins out, miles of dark ahead
And solitary cars headed for other distant cities.

## Elegy for Philip Church

Lake Superior hangs onto its submerged dead
As the legend goes, and honey-colored sunsets
Fire the birch leaves on lonely rock shores,
And you are dead now, another exhalation of cold
Raising white caps on the big lakes;
At last you are joined with breath from the pole,
Incorporeal, a wind which ruffles tern feathers
And the immaculate breasts of snow geese.
You bring things on the wind, the smell of snow
From Canada, the first roar of ice breakup
On the Beaufort. I listen for you here,
On Ohio winter afternoons at the break wall
In Cleveland, where ice stretches for miles;
You live again at the rim of pale sunsets,
A spirit of elemental cold, free and clear,
Ariel of the north, your own master again.

# The Young Marrieds

Have split apart for the weekend, like a broken
Dog bone cracked sharply on the counter edge,
Each jointed end handed to an eager dog,
The golden retriever closing gently with a soft mouth,
The German shepherd with a dangerous click of the jaws.
It was words that parted them in the middle,
She to cleave to her best friend for one
Rare, fiery autumn day, shopping, speaking
Her desires in sudden agreements; he hitting
The pedal of the electric troller digging
Bow first into fishing waters, talking waters,
Letting what lies writhing and disagreeable
Between them dry up and die in autumn sunlight.

# The Weatherman

You concern yourself with isobars
And dew points, but what I want to know is,
Can you see far enough into the heart
To predict what the weather will be there?

The old song talks about a rainy night in Georgia
When what is meant is rain in the heart,
Which is where rain doesn't easily let up—
Can you predict weather for this red soil too?

# Dark Spring Rain

If this spot were gravel paths and a great house
The day could not be more English,
Without New World weather thrown in,
No hailstones, floods or tornadoes,
Just low clouds and gentle rain
Too light to beat down the rising flowers.
Something patient is going on here,
An Old World kind of day
Lonely colonists must have yearned for
In a vast, silent, ungardened land.

## Mother

Well, Mom, you were a mighty prayer warrior
In your time, used to solving all the problems
Of the family, but my mental illness would not
Be overawed by your absolute conviction
That it was the work of the Devil alone.
I stayed bedeviled and you kept praying,
And that's the way things remained.
Who could have known it would be a small white pill
That would overcome the demons (your words)
Which drove my life without mercy,
Mightier than anything your prayers could do.
You said it then: "Doctors work God's work too."

# A Grandfather Poem

"Dad," as we called granddad, lived in the attic,
Barely shaving, drinking out of a whiskey bottle
He kept in the curved bureau drawer, which is where
I thought he kept his women (for their curves)
"Because," said my grandmother (her dewlapped cheeks
Quivering with emotion) "he and women were 'like that,'"
As she soundlessly snapped her knobby fingers.

The days come back: The lake steady with boat hum,
A palpable "childhood" summer day, wide and green
With lawns and sunlight, my grandfather sitting
On the back steps in rolled trousers and a cotton
Undershirt, his bare, part-Seminole chest flat
And ribbed like a dancer's, laughing an almost
Soundless laugh as he teased my brother, whom
He liked, and never once exchanged a word with
My grandmother, fair as a wrinkled pale bun,
Digging in her flower gardens.

Yes. The kind of summer day wide and soundless,
A searing day on the burned prairie in southern Alberta
Where nameless little rivers dig deep canyons
That expose dinosaur bones by the truckload.

A day blanked out in a blind white eye.

# The Ice Man

He propped open the thick door with a stick
And leaped on board, diving into the cool darkness
To grip each transparent, glistening block,
Huge glass bricks, lifting each gently
With the tines of his silver forceps
To swing them, as yet unbreathed, undripping
On his steady shoulder; he set the block
In the center of the dented red cooler
And began to chop it with his ice pick,
Snowing each diminishing chunk
Toward the four galvanized corners, chipping quickly
Until the chunks floated like floes, chilling
The water where they bobbed; then, lovingly,
He slipped the orange and green and brown
Bottles, the Nehi, the Royal Crown and Cotton Club
Into the ice water, plunging his bare arm to the elbow,
And filled the cooler full. After he left,
Trailing wet sawdust tracks to the screen door,
We saw the colors stacked on the bottom,
And paid, and drank, and pop exploded in our noses.

# On the Anniversary of Your Maiming

My old friend, your cartoons in high school
Had an edge of cruelty about them,
Depicting an adolescent scarecrow or fat boy
With our looks; I remember the embarrassment
I felt when you caught and nailed me,
Wriggling, to the gym wall as you passed
My picture around. When you got older
You grew remorseful, not knowing exactly
Why or for what, but then the accident happened
And part of your drawing hand was gone.
It was as if you had turned the joke on yourself
To become a permanent cartoon to the world;
Somehow, you had gotten even with yourself.

None of us who knew you would ever blame
You for your artistry. We forgot the cartoons
Along with so much else as we moved on with life,
But news of your maiming hit us hard,
And we sorrowed with you over the years,
Mourning your silent banjo gathering dust.
We knew well the cruelty that belongs to adolescence
And long ago forgave you as we joyed in you
For what you are, a good-hearted man.

# Alaska Highway

Fifty miles from Whitehorse, Yukon,
Under a clear night of stars
I picked up three drunk Indians
Hitching in the middle of the road
At 1 a.m. After giving in to the impulse
I thought sure, listening to their whiskeyed talk,
That I would be killed, tossed in a ditch
Minus my sheepskin coat and fishing money.
But the young men chatted politely
And fell asleep one by one.

When the first porch light
Appeared way off in the spruce
In the blackness on the side of the road,
I nearly wept to see it.

I dropped the boys off
At the biggest hotel in town
And gave them 20 bucks
For their next meal.

Some kinds of gratitude
Are shameful to talk about.

## Soul So Dead

Around the snarled scaly sycamores
And the dark, scaling tombstones
Ohio never ends; it grows dark
In Ohio and dawns in Ohio, as if
A city cemetery were enough of
Eternity to satisfy the generic
Man when he slips under, becomes
A grassy hollow garnished with
A small, stiff flag on the Fourth
Of July. Then the skyrockets
Make their exploding points on to
Suddenly-lit ground, and a man's
Nationality becomes more than
A coincidence of earth and birth.
Yet green or brown defines him
Better, as if all flags were
South American and obscure,
Because in death a man is known
By the grass and flowers he keeps.

# Meeting the Neighbors

She introduces herself as Allison
And "I'm three" in the same breath,
And her mother and I smile at each other.
We have found a reason to introduce ourselves,
The ice broken by a small curious daughter.
She tells me she misses the previous owners,
Misses them terribly; "They were like grandparents,"
She says, and I wonder while we talk
How we can take the place of such a sterling couple.
"They thought it was time to move," I reply,
"And their kids wanted them closer."
"I know," she says, "but my daughters need them too."
And here we are, sorrowing over the loss
Of previous owners I hardly knew, and yet knew
From the first words they spoke: Paul and Alice.
Pillars of the community. Irreplaceable.
Later, my wife looks at me steadily. "Hey, it's us now.
We live here. Let the neighbors deal with it."
And I wonder, in those seven pages of typed instructions
They left behind, did Paul and Alice explain
How we might be loved in our turn?

## Little Stars: The Radisson Hotel, April 10, 1999, Akron, Ohio

All of them dressed fit to kill, in laces and bows,
Walking just ahead of flanking purposeful parents
Who see this audition as the one which makes
Their child's career, either multiplying advertisements
Or the big roles which put their child's name
On the lips of all the show business types.
The hotel ballroom and the spotlights wait,
And no, this is not porn; it will not harness
Children to the vilest dreams men are capable of,
Nor is it child labor to help a poor country along;
The only real danger is a childhood given up to
The harsh glare of fame, which is a risk
That every doting parent here will gladly take.

## A Trip to the Airport
## For the Kindergarten Class

They bounce in, take every seat except mine,
Excited about the silvery plane they see
Hurrying down the runway, lifting into the air and flying away.
And yet, if anything in this airport is buoyant,
It is they who seem about to fly away, bouncing on their seats,
Closely imitating the sensations of flight and freedom.
A little girl spreads her arms to make wings,
And runs from window to window, shouting her excitement
At the plane, which has disappeared in low cloud cover.
Just after, their teacher gathers them up like a cluster
Of different colored balloons, holding them up by their strings,
Which they, airborne, tug against, and she watchfully carries
      them off,
Back to a day-filled room with pots and flowers.

# Dolphin

The day we caught the dolphin
The world ended for a while,
For as long as we both knew
We couldn't revive the body
Lying so seaworthy on deck.
Its length was a study
In beauty, the gray of rain clouds,
Gray of the storm-driven seas,
So used to chasing the boat,
Now unbreathing, quite still.
We washed down the shining mammal
Drowned in our net's web,
Mourned for what we didn't prevent,
Couldn't prevent; we did
The best possible thing, lifted you
Gently over the side, watched
You sink slowly out of sight.
Never again, we hoped, because
This stopped just short of murder.

# The Middle of February

Fog and snow. Just got that message
On NOAA radio, so February won't budge
And winter stays rooted to the spot.
Social Security wrote me what I've got
If I work just ten more years,
(Not enough to settle the nagging fears
About living on and dying poor
Unless I work past 70 or more—)
Thus: ground and sky so grey
They disappear, and years more to pay
For what will be coming back.
My life goes on down the slow track.

## Fishing At the Old State Park

They are all here: kids with poles, an old woman with
    shaking hands,
A bleached blonde gone to fat, cigarette hanging from
    her mouth;
A wizened black man in a lawn chair—these are the almost
    poor,
Here to fish for the price of bait, cooking the fish they catch.
The afternoon creeps by slowly, like a turtle sunning itself
On a log, undisturbed by the thrashing roll of carp in the lily
    pads.
No one moves except to fish from a new spot, gaze fixed on
    bobber
And line, and for this afternoon deprivation seems less.
Their beaters fill the parking lot, bad mufflers
Taking them home at sunset. For one day they have enough.

# Old Man In An Undershirt: Akron, Ohio, 1960

Your greasy engineer's hat sits high on your forehead,
But your belly has settled well below the belt,
And you are comfortable now with fishing pole
    and plastic bucket,
Gently closing the trunk of your undercoated car
Too generic to come up with make or model,
But a good fit for you, preferring namelessness
Out here at the state park where fishing by yourself
Is how the local folks do it. The stink of rubber shops
Downtown is far away, at least two beers down the road,
Or if a weekend, forty-eight hours away;
You'll take your fish home and eat them
Fried in cornmeal and Crisco, or give them
To your black neighbor down the street.
The whole week is carbon black and sweat, carbon black
    and sweat,
But out here the world is more kindly,
Offering up long spells of quiet water,
Cruising mallards and unhurried cigarettes.

# What Is A Dog's Life

First, an appetite
Coming to look at its bowl.
Claws clacking on the kitchen floor.

A black nose thrust out
As the front door starts to open!

Then, a greeting, with sounds of joy
And much stretching after the day shift
Guarding the living room.

A persistent whine to throw the ball.
Throw the ball, throw the ball again!

A sniffing front and back
When stranger dogs intrude.

At eight years a twisted intestine,
Emergency surgery and one cranky bite—
The terse note "Bites" on the recovery cage!

At thirteen loyal years a quiet death
With those whom a dog loves present.
A burial beneath the lilac bush in bloom,
Near Daisy's grave, the first dog.

A fond good-bye as the dog's body
Is placed carefully in the hole.

Left behind: A deep place in your owner's thoughts
Long after. And for always: a permanent home.

# Jim's Meadow

Jim's meadow is simply a green hilltop
Behind three shores, Rex Lake, in front
Of Turkeyfoot Lake, in front of Mud
Lake. The meadow sits way back,
The only pastoral hillside above
A heavily cottaged, heavily wooded
Chain of lakes. It is not a significant
Meadow, except that it belonged
To Jim Crouse, who left it in his
Wife's keeping when he was taken
Suddenly with a heart attack;
It still has the name attached,
And it was a known destination
For every kid who picked up a canoe
Paddle. Jim followed his parents'
Wishes and hung onto the farm,
Resisting the considerable money
Of lake developers; his land gave
The rest of us assurance that
One place would keep its name;
It's been more than a year now
And no yellow machines have crawled
Down the hill, scraping as they go—
What his wife does with the farm
Is none of our business, really,
But the hay meadow is still there,
Reminding us that Jim spent
Some time on this earth defending
The meadow from the incursions
Of developers, as his father did
Before him, and it must have been
Harder for Jim; now, in my mind,

The meadow comes to stand for Jim,
Takes on his features of patience
And decency, as if a meadow could
Be decent, yet somehow the greenscape
Everybody knows is a solid, an
Immovable, and a decent thing;
It gives comfort and assurance
To kids growing up around the lake,
Who care less about real estate values;
Besides, the white picket fence
Follows the curve of the hill up
To the house, which is screened
On three sides, a gracious place.
Jim had two college-age kids
Who might end up doing the same
Thing, hanging on to the farm
Too; what a temptation to sell,
Though. But maybe that is just
My failure of faith; they might
Feel the same way about the farm
As Jim does, whose motives were
As clear as the minnows darting
Across the sandy bottom of the lake, and as
Comforting to us as they were
To him, no doubt; we still depend
On Jim to be stronger than we
Would be, which is the usual
Unfairness of neighbors; we'll
Probably go on depending on Jim
And Jim's kids to be better,
Stronger, than we would ever be,
And go on depending on the meadow
Being there, because we know
From childhood that neighbors, at least
The good ones, never fail.

## Academic Trip: Leaving The Dog Behind

Your philosopher master
Has gone off to India
Leaving you alone

In your Alaska
Where winter will come on
And the snow chest deep

Will be your day's walk,
Which you have always loved.
Thinking dust and heat,

Your master will change
His shirts and shorts twice a day
And dream of blue snow.

## School Buses

Six of them: great orange, great golden carp
Lined up at the railroad crossing, red stop fins fanning.
Each waits, each listens, and crosses in turn
Headed for the lily shoals of children.

# Classroom Visual

"Poetry is just enough,"
Stuart told us,
Balancing carefully
On the rock in the middle of the stream
In the classroom,
"Without falling in," he said.

I tend to think I would
Build bridges, overdo it—

The white-haired poet
Skipped from one wet rock
To the next and landed safely
On the other side,

And we marveled:
His feet were dry.

## Checkout Lines At The Grocery Store

Old woman, you make no effort to open your purse
While your groceries are being rung up,
And when you do, it is money to the penny,
Every coin fished out of your coin purse,
And then, register tape in hand,
You stand there as if addled
Until the high school-aged bagger
Offers to push your cart to your car.

In the meantime I am tied in knots
Waiting for this ritual to end,
But what saves me from saying anything
Is a picture of you humbly preparing
Your food, thanking God for the little needed
To keep you alive, and in your prayer
Still wishing you had a husband to cook for.
I find myself praying too, against all casual annoyance.

## Autumn Rain

Dark November morning,
Swift gutter floods
And the dark shine
Of children's rain gear
In street lamps,
Children who follow
The swirl
Of street water
To its underworld
Descent, or stand
Booted in the stream
Idly testing the
Current with a stick.

## Beluga Swim Up The Kasilof River While The Fleet Sits At Anchor, Asleep

Stretched stillness as the current runs,
The boats taut on their anchors;
Ghostly white, the mammal shapes flow past,
Pushing current and moonlight upriver;
They roll under slowly, then back up, their Beluga tails
Folding in like a spoon in cake mix.
Feeding ghosts, their gleaming backs and sides
Crowd the mud banks,
Veer around the old barge humming with
Diesel generator to the bleached night,
Vapor lights bright on dun steel decks.
Somewhere ahead, anchored boats sit too thick
To pass, tied six together on their orange steel buoys
And the sixteen-footers turn back,
Dive and surface slowly out to
The daylight business of open sea.
In here anchors drag and money means.

# Ice Fishing

They drive up after the first shift, the early ones,
Friends, fathers with sons, solitary old guys,
Wearing Oshkosh overalls, winter camouflage suits,
White stuttered with black lines as if they were
Snow and bush, or snow and tree branch, and carrying
Long augers, the jumbo size of brace and bit
For some winter carpentering, and buckets, always
Buckets to carry the bait and the fish.
Some put up dark green or solid blue nylon huts,
Setting them up like tents, dragging them across
The ice on wooden runners, like kids pulling their
Sleds slowly up a hill, and they go out where
Boats have been in summer, now a solid footing
On a solid state, the grey ice hidden in deep
Snowfall, but in the hissing, brightly-lit warmth
The little rod tip bends and jerks, and the
Shining, newly-minted fish freeze quickly in air,
Refrigerate on bluish twilight snow, and all
Of this is logical, for a purpose, written
About in the fishing columns, as if the
Shining moon and the ghostly golf links
Across the channel had lost their logic,
And sitting with cold feet in winter air
Were no longer sport, but life's only purpose,
As long on instinct as the best fairway shot.

# Alaska: John's Song

So it was tapes, eight-track tapes all the way back
From a day's fishing, good music, and a few beers
To cut the soreness as the high bluffs on shore
Rose up to meet us, promising calm water and rest,
The time for unloading, for counting up the catch,
And a quick sink into tired, satisfied sleep.

We knew how rich we were going to be by the fish
In the hold; every fish meant groceries or lumber,
A plane ticket out, a new bicycle, new clothes,
Not that we wore new clothes much, but the kids
Had school, and we all had family to visit.
The sea's bounty kept us throughout the wide year.

Life outside of fishing was all dry land stuff,
Towns and mountains, back roads, big and small parks,
The Canadian border, wheat fields and black oil rigs,
Sometimes a good hotel, and late restaurant breakfasts.
To have enough to live on freed all the rest of the time
Until the fishing started again and drew us back.

Those days are almost gone, just as the fish are gone,
Just as the kids grow up to graduate, just as wives separate,
Just as the time to save a marriage gets away.
You lived your lives, took what the land and sea offered,
Lived as young people do, dividing clear to the marrow,
And savored everything that was sweet about your lives.

Did we use the land, or did this quiet land use us?
The sea shines, the mountain peaks dazzle in white,
The fireweed purples, a royal color, in roadside ditches
Whether we are there or not. We can no longer help it;
Our bones mutter with age, and the cold sinks in.
Now we envy the strong and young ones
Who come after us.

## A Letter To My Education Majors

I think I will give advice, which I always shunned,
But I've gotten to that age now that wants
To leave something, some kernel of wisdom, behind.
What shall I tell you—long hours and low pay?
You already know that. How about sullen students
Who hate to go home at night for reasons
It would shake our calm to know about—
You will get students like that, and you
Will be the one, if you are lucky, they turn to.
Don't miss the chance to help, even if
You are feeling particularly helpless; you can't
Change the world, can't eliminate the savagery
Which breaks or tempers kids in its
All-consuming fire, but your classroom
Can be a haven of sorts, where you have to
Draw the line in the sand which
The dangerous beast on the other side
Will probably dare to cross. If I could,
I would wrap you all in armour of light
Because truth comes hard, and dark motives
Hate the light. You will find this out.
And one more thing—we cannot pick our battles;
They pick us, so be ready for the unexpected,
And try not to grow too complacent,
No, not even after years of service,
Because calm won't stay that way.
So that's it. You will listen, or not,
Just as you like, while your career awaits you.
Take love with you as you go,
For you will need it all, and more,
To feed the hungry hearts of kids
You teach. Now I've said enough. God speed.

## First Snow

The brightness hurting the eyes
Lies just outside, the size
Of snowy fields as far as
One can see in this county,
Where snow blooms driving east.
This is winter's bounty
Clean and spare, the least
Of the season's snowfalls,
White fields in blue air.

# Acknowledgments

The author and publisher make grateful acknowledgments to the following publications in which these poems first appeared.

*Pudding*: "The Young Marrieds," "Dark Spring Rain," "Alaska Highway," "Soul So Dead," "Autumn Rain," and "Ice Fishing"

*Pleiades*: "The Poet's Function," "A Grandfather Poem"

*Iconoclast*: "Jim's Meadow"

*Learning By Heart*: "School Buses"

*Canto*: "Classroom Visual," and "Beluga Swim Up The Kasilof River While The Fleet Sits at Anchor, Asleep"

*Mobius*: "Alaska: John's Song"

*Calliope*: "A Letter To My Education Majors"

---

Cover art, "Ice Fishing" (1887) signed by Northrop G. Matthews, is used courtesy of the Freshwater and Marine Image Bank located in the University of Washington Libraries.